Designed by: Ryan Snow and SnowStudios   www.snowstudiosla.com

Compiled and edited by: Meghan Dowd, Rachana Rathi, and Matthew Scharpnick

Special thanks to: Ben Henretig, Daniel Moss, Gopika Prabhu, and Niraj Shekar

TABLE OF CONTENTS

Introduction

Sri Sri Ravi Shankar is a walking example of what it means to live "Life @ 100%."

A global humanitarian and spiritual leader, Sri Sri inspires millions of people worldwide with his indelible wit, wisdom and love.

His brilliance lies in his simplicity.

Sri Sri makes profound truths accessible – and relevant – to people of every age, race, religion and culture; and he provides practical ways to apply this wisdom in everyday life.

This book is no different. A compilation of talks by Sri Sri, it touches on topics at the center of young lives: success, relationships and how to make a difference in the world.

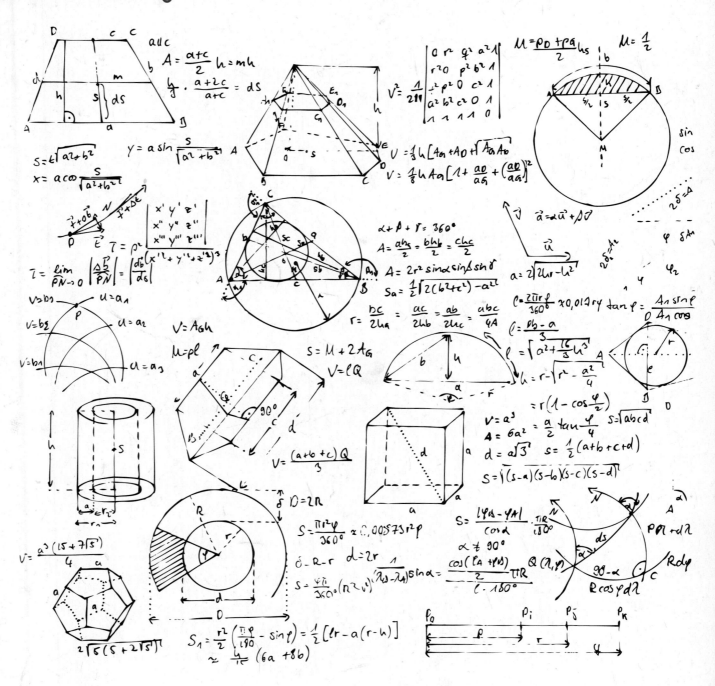

The Purpose of Knowledge

The purpose of knowledge is to make you feel you don't know.

If knowledge makes you feel like you know it all, then it has not fulfilled its goal.

The more you know, the more you become aware of the unknown.

Being in an innocent state of wonder, of "I don't know!", you feel the mind becoming quiet. This makes life simple and wonderful.

success at

100%

What is Success?

Success is measured by the strength of your smile. It is the confidence you have to face challenges.

[**True success is smiling even when everything falls apart.**]

When everything goes well, it is easy to smile.

True success is smiling even when everything falls apart.

Secret of Success

Success requires you to focus on others, not yourself.

This may contradict what you understand to be success. Usually you think of success as getting what you want out of life.

If you only think of yourself, your vision, creativity and motivation will always be restricted by your personal situation.

However, if you look at any successful entrepreneur, athlete or social leader, they are successful because they understand what others want. Success is a byproduct of considering the needs of people.

If you only think of yourself, your vision, creativity and motivation will always be restricted by your personal situation. It is easy to get frustrated when you are only thinking about yourself.

> # When you think of others, your focus expands, vision broadens and creativity grows.

However, you will move toward lasting success if you step back and ask, "What is needed in the world? What do others need to be happy, more comfortable and content?"

When you think of others, your focus expands, vision broadens and creativity grows. And success – no matter how you define it – will come to you on its own.

Limit-Less

When you do something beyond your perceived limits, you claim it as an achievement, a success. You do not celebrate success when something is well within your capability.

> **Assuming a limit is underestimating yourself. You are creating your own roadblocks and obstacles.**

You do not say you successfully drank a glass of water because it is within your capabilities. But when you do something that is beyond your perceived limits, you claim it as success.

If success means crossing a limit, it assumes you have a limit. Yet, assuming a limit is underestimating yourself. You are creating your own roadblocks and obstacles.

When you realize your unbounded potential, no action is really an achievement. All your gains and achievements can only be smaller than you.

(Focus on possibilities rather than achievements. And realize you are beyond the limits placed on you by society, friends and even yourself.)

Anyone who claims to be successful only reveals his limitations. If you feel very successful, it means that you have underestimated yourself.

Focus on possibilities rather than achievements. And realize you are beyond the limits placed on you by society, friends and even yourself.

There is no question of success if you have nothing to gain. There is nothing to gain if you have only come to give and serve.

When you realize you are limitless, no action is an achievement.

Be Fearless

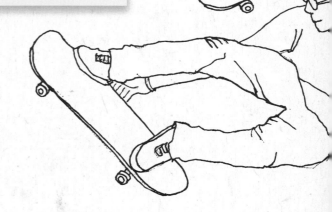

When you take actions based only on convenience, you compromise the quality of your work.

The most successful people in the world do things regardless of how they feel.

Often you say, "I just don't feel like doing this." Then, when it has to get done, you rush and cut corners to finish.

The most successful people in the world do things regardless of how they feel. They move based on their commitments, and they strive to get things done right.

When you are adventurous, creative or truly passionate about a goal, it breeds commitment.

However, there is a balance. If you are totally trapped by a commitment, if it is too inconvenient too often, you get frustrated and burn out.

When you are adventurous, creative or truly passionate about a goal, it breeds commitment. You cannot even consider convenience. Your commitment comes naturally.

Whatever you are committed to brings you strength.

If you are committed to your family, then your family supports you. If you are committed to society, you enjoy the support of society. If you are committed to God, God gives you strength. If you are committed to Truth, Truth brings you strength.

Often you are not aware of this and hesitate to commit to a greater cause. You are afraid commitment will weaken you or take away your freedom.

Your commitment to a cause will bring you greater comfort in the long run.

Education:
What's the Big Idea?

Is education only about getting good grades to get a good job? Or is it about laying the foundation for long-term prosperity of society as a whole?

> A truly well educated person is friendly, compassionate and capable of selfless action.

True education is more than what lies in the books. It gives you the life skills necessary to attain your dreams. A truly well educated person is friendly, compassionate and capable of selfless action.

A complete education incorporates knowledge about the world's cultures and religions, as well as knowledge about the mind and how to manage negative emotions.

A complete education empowers you to play the role of a global citizen, making the local community stronger and the world a safer and happier place to live.

The Strong Can Work for a Fool

A lot of people do not want to work under someone. The general notion is that when you work under someone, you lose your freedom.

[One who knows his own strength can work effectively even under a fool.]

People often want to start their own business out of a desire to be their own boss. Yet, to succeed in business, you are accountable to everyone you deal with. If you cannot be accountable to even one person, how can you be accountable to many? This is the paradox.

Refusing to work under someone is a sign of weakness, not strength. A strong person feels comfortable working under someone because he knows his strength. The weak and poor in spirit do not like to work under anyone else because they are unaware of their own strength. They cannot be successful in business nor in any profession.

The same is true even in community service. Often volunteers do not want to work under someone else. This is merely an exhibition of their weakness. With such an attitude, they achieve very little.

One who is timid and weak in spirit would be uncomfortable to work even under a wise one, but one who knows his own strength can work effectively even under a fool.

Doing vs. Happening

Only one who is 100% in action can recognize life is a happening.

The healthiest way to live is to see the whole past as a happening and the present as doing.

If you see the past as doing, then ego and regret come along.

Let "everything is a happening" apply to the past. Let action be in the present.

When you see the present as happening, it brings laziness and a lack of awareness.

If you see action in the future, it brings tension and worry.

If you apply "happening" to the future, it brings some confidence and also some lethargy.

Let "everything is a happening" apply to the past. Let action be in the present. The future is a mix of both.

The wise will see the doing in happening and the happening in doing simultaneously.

One who does a lot of work will never say they did a lot. When someone says they did a lot of work, it usually means they can do more. They haven't done enough.

Being humble is less stressful than constantly showing everyone what you have accomplished. "Doer-ship" is tiring.

Remember, all of your talents are for others. If you have a good voice, it is for others. If you are a good cook, it is for others. If you write a good book, it is for others. You don't sit and read your own book. You cannot perform surgery on yourself.

All of your work and talents are for others.

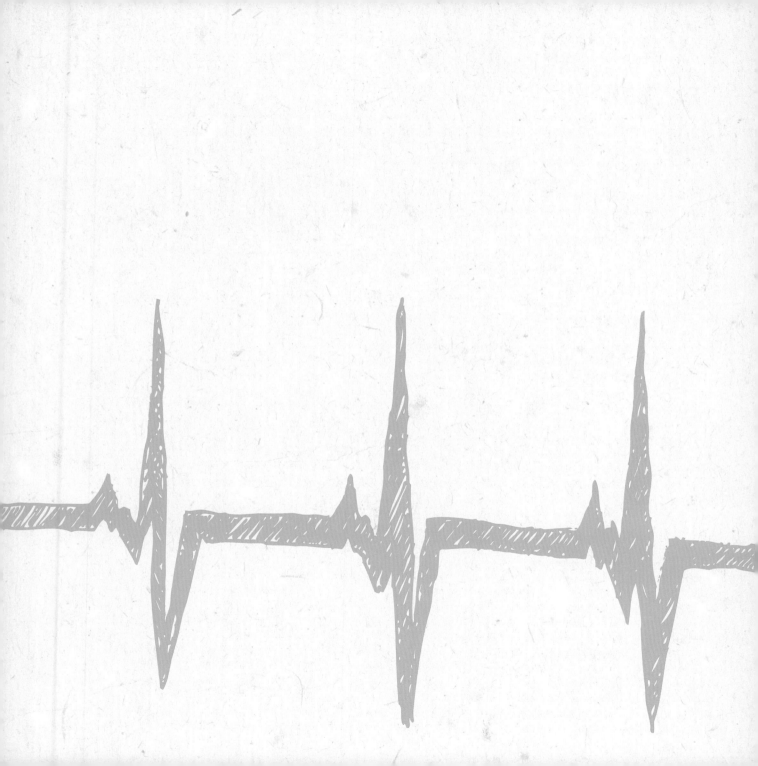

Health at

100%

A Perfect State of Health

What does it mean to be healthy?

We hear about physical and dental hygiene, but rarely about mental hygiene.

> To attain a perfect state of health, you have to be mentally calm and steady.

Our mind is like a container. We are simply dumping things into it and not attend to its cleanliness. Stress accumulates, and in turn, depletes our health.

If your mind is stiff, you are not mentally healthy. When your emotions are rough, you are not emotionally healthy.

To attain a perfect state of health, you have to be mentally calm and steady. Mental well-being manifests in clear perception, observation and expression.

Clear the system of stress and keep your energy level high through mind-body activities such as breathing techniques, meditation and yoga.

The practice of yoga releases tension and negative emotions, and helps you live in the present moment. Meditation is food for your soul and it brings forth an inner wealth. Meditation is a hundred times more refreshing than sleep. It effortlessly brings you to the present moment, freeing you from anger about the past and worry about the future.

Practices such as yoga, pranayama (breathing practices) and meditation provide physical, emotional and mental health. This is true wealth, true health.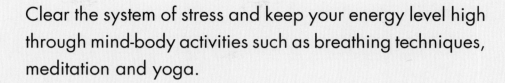

Health is not merely the absence of disease. It is the dynamic expression of life.

One very simple way to relax and get more energy is to practice alternate nostril breathing. Here you use your right hand to plug one nostril at a time. Using the inside of your ring finger plug your left nostril and breathe out through your right nostril. Then breathe in through your right nostril, plug it with your thumb, and breathe out through your left nostril. You can continue for a few minutes taking relaxed long breaths in one nostril, plugging it, and then out the other nostril. Afterward just sit for a minute or two with eyes closed, or meditate for longer if you wish. ❧

Sources of Energy

Stress and tension obstruct human values.

When you are tense, your perception, observation and expression suffer.

You can be free of tension either by lessening your workload or increasing your energy level. Lessening your workload is often not an option, so how can you increase energy?

There are four main sources of energy:

1. Food: Food influences your mind, thoughts and behavior. It is important to get the right type and right amount of food.

2. Sleep: When you sleep too little, you tend to be cranky and slower mentally. When you get too much sleep, you feel dull. A good amount of sleep, not too much and not too little, is important.

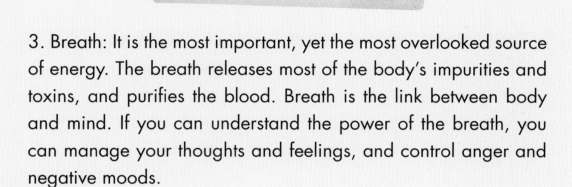

3. Breath: It is the most important, yet the most overlooked source of energy. The breath releases most of the body's impurities and toxins, and purifies the blood. Breath is the link between body and mind. If you can understand the power of the breath, you can manage your thoughts and feelings, and control anger and negative moods.

[You can be free of tension either by lessening your workload or increasing your energy levels.]

4. Happy, meditative mind: A meditative mind gives you so much energy. Have you ever noticed that you can work around the clock without getting tired when you are working on projects you love? But when you are at the office or doing homework, even two hours exhaust you? The state of your mind plays an important role in your energy level. ⚘

Promise of Pleasure

What lies behind every desire? A wish to be happy.

Happiness is the goal of every desire. But how often does a desire lead you to your goal?

Desires only postpone happiness. They indicate this moment is not okay, and joy is somewhere off in the future.

But joy is never tomorrow; it can only be experienced now, in this moment.

Desires only *appear* to lead you to happiness. They are just a promise of pleasure.

You have no control over desires. Even if you say, "Oh, I shouldn't be desiring…" that is another desire! Asking, "When will I be free of desires?" is another desire.

Recognize your desires as they come and let go. This will help you remain centered. Then nothing can shake you.

Otherwise small things can upset you or make you sad. You become upset over what? A few words from here or there, or some insult makes you sad?

(fragile peace is of no use.)

As long as desires linger in your mind, your mind cannot be at total rest.

Recognizing how small desires really are, seeing they are nothing to be bothered by – this is maturity.

As a child, you got tired of your toys and wanted new toys. Then you got tired of playing with the new toys, and wanted to play with people. As a teenager, it was about something else, like watching a new movie or wearing the coolest clothes.

Later, you start searching for a spouse, a companion. You get married. You make a very good couple. Then what? You want your own home, children, family. Those who are single think married people are better off. Those who are married think single people are better off.

Look at your whole life. It is the desire that tires you, the 'want' in the mind. Your mind tires you more than physical work.

If you are willing to do some work, even 15 hours at a stretch will not tire you. However, if you are not willing and you have to work for even two hours, it will tire you.

✳ Thinking you need rest makes you restless.

✳ Thinking you have to work hard makes you tired.

✳ Thinking you have worked hard brings self-pity.

When you are tired, small things can irritate you and can throw you off balance. Our peace is so fragile that anything, even a phone call, can throw it off. Our sense of peace breaks into a thousand pieces with just a few words from someone. Fragile peace is of no use.

The peace and love in our life should be so solid, like a diamond. Nothing should be able to shake it.

Overcoming Addiction & Obsessions

There are three ways to overcome addiction and obsessions:

Love: By promising your parents, close friends or yourself that you will quit the habit – you will be able to get rid of it. This is the best way.

Greed: If you were promised a million dollars to quit for six months, will you still be addicted?

Fear: The fear of an ailment, debilitation, etc. will not allow you to stay addicted.

Your inability to do something, like break a habit, causes a pinch, and when you are deeply pained by something, the pain will rid you of that habit.

Along with these three ways, practice yoga and pranayama (breathing techniques).

And take a vow you will not indulge in addictions. This vow should be time bound, and consider the appropriate time and place to take the vow.

Suppose someone has a habit of smoking cigarettes and says, "I will quit smoking," but cannot do it. He can take a time-bound vow for 90 days. If you have a habit of cursing and swearing, take a vow not to use bad language for 10 days.

Do not take the vow for a lifetime or you will break it immediately. If you happen to break it before the time has elapsed, don't worry. Just begin again. Slowly increase the duration until it becomes your nature.

Your inability to do something, like break a habit, causes a pinch and when you are deeply pained by something, the pain will rid you of that habit.

If you are pained by your shortcomings, then you are a seeker. Pain takes you out of addiction.

Know the Impermanence of the World

Many people are anxious about how to deal with their anxiety. Here are some ways you can manage your anxiety:

1. Sing, dance and celebrate. The very intention to celebrate will pull you away from anxiety to a more harmonious state.

2. Think about what you can do for others rather than just yourself. Energize yourself with some community service.

Invoke the lion within you.

3. Practice yoga, breathing and meditation.

4. Know the impermanence of the world. See that everything is changing.

5. Have faith and surrender to the Divine. Know there is a supreme

power who loves you. The supreme power is behind you and accepts you totally. This sense of security comes with the sense of belonging.

6. Invoke your valor/courage. Invoke the lion within you and have an attitude of sacrifice. This will rescue you from anxiety.

7. Remind yourself that you are committed to a greater goal.

8. Be unpredictable for a while. Anxiety is always related to some anticipated action. Do something completely irrelevant and unpredictable.

9. Be willing to face the worst. This will leave you with stability in the mind.

10. Remember a similar situation in the past when you were able to overcome your anxiety.

Relationships at 100%

When you want love, the
want itself can delay love
from manifesting.

Love is Your Nature

Know that love is a gift. You can't force anyone to feel love. Your craving to feel love becomes a hindrance to feeling love. Just relax.

When you want love, the want itself can delay love from manifesting. All you need to do is let go and relax. You will see your nature is love. Love is always there when you are relaxed and easygoing.

And it will manifest when it should. For instance, the sun is always there, but it rises at its own time right? The sun does not shine here all the time, even though it exists 24/7 and is shining in some part of the world at every moment.

In the same way, all the beautiful feelings in your life are there with you all the time. You can't forcefully manifest them. They will manifest at different times in life.

Relax and take them as they come.

Sustaining Relationships

Here are a few tips to make your relationships stronger and more successful:

1. In every relationship, there is give and take. Give more and take less. If you only give, you will make the other person feel obligated and they will feel uncomfortable being with you. If you only take, you will become like a parasite and the relationship will die a quick death. See to it that you give. And when you give, don't give half-heartedly. Give generously.

> See to it that you give. And when you give, don't give halfheartedly. Give generously.

And remember to take anything given to you graciously. This will ensure the other person will never feel obligated to you. Your relationship will be healthy. Both people in the relationship should come from a place of giving. If both only want to take, then there will be fights and rifts. Both should focus on giving.

2. Focus on the positive aspects of the relationship. In any relationship, there will be negative and positive things. For the relationship to grow, keep your focus on the good things. Remember the reasons why you came together in the first place, and keep coming back to those in difficult times. Your relationship will bloom and blossom.

3. When one of you becomes angry or upset, the other should keep their cool. Let the other person blow off their temper. Be compassionate and considerate. If both people in the relationship simultaneously lose their cool, then the relationship will break up very fast. When both people in the relationship meditate regularly, this happens very rarely.

[Don't ask for proof that the other person loves you.]

4. Don't ask for proof that the other person loves you. Take it for granted that the other person loves you. If they have to prove their love to you over and over again, it is exhausting.

For a seed to sprout, you cannot leave it on the surface or bury it too deep in the ground. It needs to be just at the right place below the surface to sprout and grow. In the same way, expressing your love too much or too little will hamper the growth of your relationship. Keep the dignity of your love.

⇨ Sometimes heartbreak is inevitable.

5. Keep your focus on something big, not on each other. If you only focus on each other, you will start to find faults in no time. And "I cannot live without him" will quickly change into "I cannot live with him!"

   Many couples start to fight once their children grow and become independent. Until then, they both focused on the well-being of their children. Once that is no longer needed, the focus shifts to each other and they begin to find faults. Keeping the focus on something bigger helps heal a stressful relationship tremendously.

6. Sometimes heartbreak is inevitable. Move on. There will be pain and time will heal it. Meditation will give you strength. Doing community service will also help you get out of the pain much faster. It can heal you sooner than you expect. ❧

Smile in the Face of Rudeness

What do you do when someone is rude to you?

- Get annoyed
- Be rude to them
- Get upset
- Run away from and avoid the person or the situation
- Blame the person
- Preach to the person

None of these will strengthen you.

Instead, see rude behavior in a different light:

- It indicates the intensity of their commitment
- It indicates their stress and insensitivity
- It projects their upbringing
- It indicates a behavioral pattern
- It shows a lack of understanding
- It shows a lack of observation of their own mind

- It shows you behavior to avoid
- It is an opportunity for you to welcome and absorb the rudeness
- It strengthens your mind

The next time someone is rude to you, make sure you don't get upset. Just smile back. If you can digest the rudeness, then nothing whatsoever can shake you. 🍃

Coping with Loss

Isn't the mind ruling your body? When you drive a car, what is moving the car: the body or the mind? If the mind is not in the body, the body alone cannot do anything. The body, without the mind, will be six feet underground.

Meditation has the ability to annihilate the fear of death.

The formless is ruling your life. The formless is ruling the world. And there is a greater formlessness that is ruling the entire universe. Call it whatever you want: God, Consciousness or Energy. You are the center of that greater formlessness.

In many cultures, when someone dies, people take 10 days to be totally in that void and meditate. Meditation happens easily

during this time period. Meditation is very similar to this experience of void. In meditation, you realize you are not just the body. You are more than the body.

Clean your slate with meditation.

Meditation has the ability to annihilate the fear of death. Meditation is like cleaning the slate. Your slate, your consciousness, has so many things written on it.

If you are going to write on it again, you have to wipe it clean. Otherwise, you begin to overwrite, and overwrite, and overwrite, and then you cannot read anything on it! Life is a mess when your mind has been overwritten so many times, with one impression on top of the other.

Clean your slate with meditation.

Fools Get Together

People with similar tendencies come together. Intelligent people group together, fools get together, happy people get together, ambitious people get together and disgruntled people also group together and glorify their problems.

> A wise person feels at home with the disgruntled as well as the happy, foolish and intelligent.

When disgruntled people get together, they complain about everything and pull each other down. A frustrated person cannot be with someone happy because they are not on the same wavelength.

A wise person feels at home with the disgruntled as well as the happy, foolish and intelligent. Similarly, people with all of these tendencies also feel at home with the wise.

Take a look around and see what goes in your group of friends — are you grateful or grumbling? Take responsibility to uplift the people around you.

A wise person is like the sky where all birds can fly.

Humor and Humiliation

Humor is a buffer that saves you from humiliation. If you have a good sense of humor, you can never be humiliated.

Humor brings everyone together, while humiliation tears them apart. In a society torn by humiliation and insult, humor is like a breath of fresh air. A good sense of humor relieves you from fear and anxiety.

Humor should be coupled with care and concern. Humor without care and concern, as well as appropriate action, often irritates those who come to you with serious problems.

The wise use humor to bring wisdom and to lighten every situation.
The intelligent use humor as a shield against humiliation.
The cruel use humor as a sword to insult others.
The irresponsible use humor to escape from responsibility.
And fools take humor too seriously!

How do you cultivate a sense of humor?

1. Humor is not just words, it is the lightness of your being. You do not have to read and repeat jokes. Being cordial and lighthearted brings out authentic humor.

2. Don't take life too seriously (you will never come out of it alive!)

3. Have a sense of belonging with everybody, including those who are not friendly

4. Practice yoga and meditation

5. Have unshakable faith

6. Be in the company of those who live in knowledge and are humorous

7. Be willing to be a clown

Every Day is New

When you are full of prana, or energy, you see:

All that happened until this moment is gone – finished. The past is gone. Everything that happened, happened.

Your mind is in the present moment, and you are able to think of what to do now.

Sometimes 100% of your actions will be successful. Other times, not. A farmer knows that not every seed he sows will sprout. He throws the seeds into the field anyway. He doesn't worry that this seed will sprout and this one won't sprout.

From now on, today is a new chapter. Every day is a new chapter. Bring up this awareness again and again.

The Essence of Religion

There is a crisis facing the world today. It is primarily one of identification.

People identify themselves with limited characteristics such as gender, race, religion and nationality, forgetting their basic identity

[**The highest identification we can make is that we are part of Divinity.**]

as part of the entire existence. These limited identifications lead to conflict on both a global and personal level.

Every individual is much more than the sum of these limited identifications. The highest identification we can make is that we are part of Divinity (pure energy or whatever you choose to call it).

And secondly, we are human beings and members of the human family. In divine creation, the human race, as a whole, is united.

Religion has three aspects: values, rituals and symbols. Moral and spiritual values are common to all traditions. The symbols and practices – those rituals and customs that form a way of life within a religion – distinguish one tradition from another and give each of them a unique charm.

Symbols and practices are like the banana skin. The spiritual values – the quest for truth and awareness of our divinity – are the banana. However, in every tradition, most people have thrown away the banana and are holding onto the banana skin.

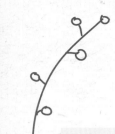

The Greatest Wealth

Faith is a great wealth. It is a blessing.

If you lack faith, you have to pray for faith. But to pray, you need faith. This is a paradox.

> There are three types of faith: faith in yourself, faith in the world, and faith in something higher.

There are three types of faith: faith in yourself, faith in the world, and faith in something higher.

You need to have faith in yourself. Without faith, you think, "I can't do this. This is not for me. I will never be free in this life."

You must have faith in the world. Without this, you can't move an inch in the world. Banks give you loans with the faith that you will pay them back. You deposit money in the bank with the faith it will be returned. If you doubt everything in the world, nothing will happen.

Happiness springs forth from faith.

The same is the case with faith in the Divine. Have faith in the Divine and you will evolve.

All these faiths are connected. You must have all three for each of them to be strong.

On the other hand, people have faith in the world, but the whole world is just a soap bubble, an illusion in which everything is changing all the time. People have faith in themselves, but they don't know who they are. People think that they have faith in God, but they have no idea of God.

In science, faith follows knowledge. In spirituality, knowledge follows faith.

For example, the knowledge that pesticides and chemical fertilizers are good for plants came from science, so people had faith in them and used them all over the world. Then, new knowledge said they were not good and people's faith shifted to organic farming.

Knowledge brought faith, the knowledge changed and then the faith changed. The knowledge and faith of science is of "happening."

In spirituality, faith is first and knowledge comes later. For example, if you do yoga faithfully then you attain knowledge of the significance of yoga. If you do your meditation faithfully, the knowledge of a greater consciousness follows. Even an illiterate person, through faith, can attain deep wisdom.

If you think you are doing God a favor by having faith in God, you are mistaken. Faith gives you strength instantaneously. Faith brings you stability, clarity, calmness and love.

When you lack faith, you cannot find happiness in the inner or outer world.

What is Meditation?

A mind in the present moment is meditation. A mind without agitation is meditation. A mind that moves beyond thought is meditation. A mind that has no hesitation and no anticipation is meditation. A mind that has come back home to its true source is meditation.

A mind in the present moment is meditation.

Total rest is meditation. Only when the mind settles down can total rest happen. Restlessness, agitation, desire and ambition stir up the mind and keep it busy in planning for the future or being regretful and angry about the past. Real freedom is freedom from the past and future.

Wakefulness is a state of consciousness in which there is alertness but no rest. If you stay awake too long, you feel tired. Sleep is a state of consciousness in which there is rest, but no alertness. Dreams are a state of consciousness in which there is neither rest nor alertness. If you have too many dreams, you wake up and say you didn't have a very deep sleep.

There is a fourth state of consciousness: the meditative state. In a meditative state, there is full alertness and deep, deep rest. Meditation is like a flight to outer space where there is no sunset and no sunrise, nothing but a void.

The delicate art of doing nothing is meditation. You may sit with eyes closed, but if desires keep arising, you are only fooling yourself into thinking you are meditating. You are just daydreaming.

Letting go of thoughts and desires as they arise is a skill that needs to be learned from an expert teacher. When you can learn to let go, you will be joyful. As you start being joyful, more will be given to you. That is meditation.

Rest and activity are opposite values, but they compliment each other. The deeper you are able to rest, the more dynamic you can be in activity. Hanging on to planning can hold you back from diving deep in meditation. Just this understanding is good enough.

Let go, sit and see how a few days of meditation practice can change the quality of your life. 🌿

Silence is the Goal

Some questions can be answered only in silence.

Silence is the goal of all answers. If an answer does not silence the mind, it is not an answer.

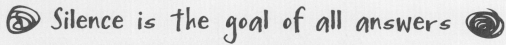 **Silence is the goal of all answers**

Thoughts are not the goal. The goal of thoughts is silence.

When you contemplate on the question "Who am I?", you don't get an answer, there is silence. That is the real answer, for your soul is solidified silence. This solidified silence is wisdom; it is knowledge.

The easy way to silence thoughts is to arouse feelings. For through feelings, peace, joy and love dawn. And they are all your very nature.

To the question "Who am I?", the only relevant answer is silence. You need to discard all other answers and hold on to the question: "Who am I?" All other answers are just thoughts. Thoughts can never be complete.

Only silence is complete.

The Only Thing
You Must Remember

The only thing you must remember is how fortunate you are.

When you forget how fortunate you are, it leads to sadness.

The purpose of sorrow is to bring you back to the Self. And the Self is all joy. But coming back to the Self is possible only through knowledge or self-awareness.

With the power of knowledge, you transcend sorrow.

Knowledge or awareness leads sorrow toward the Self. Without knowledge, the same sorrow multiplies. With the power of knowledge, you transcend sorrow.

We have this beautiful knowledge which has all the flavors in it – wisdom, laughter, service, silence, singing, dancing, humor, celebration, caring, complaints, problems, complications and some chaos (to add color).

Life is so colorful. Be grateful.

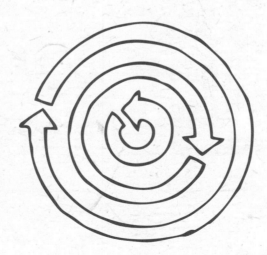

About H.H. Sri Sri Ravi Shankar and the Art of Living Foundation

Founded by Sri Sri Ravi Shankar in 1981, the Art of Living Foundation is an educational and humanitarian non-profit organization active in more than 140 countries.

Sri Sri, a global humanitarian and spiritual leader, created Art of Living with a mission to create a Violence-Free, Stress-Free world – one individual at a time.

Today, the Foundation is the world's largest volunteer driven non-governmental organization.

Art of Living's self-development workshops and trauma and disaster relief programs have impacted the lives of more than 25 million people, who range from underprivileged high school students, political leaders and farmers to Ivy League students, prisoners, housewives and corporate executives.

Sri Sri travels to more than 40 countries a year, spreading his message of peace and compassion. He has created hundreds of schools and organizations to serve the needs of humanity.

Among Sri Sri's initiatives are YES and YES Plus, innovative leadership workshops designed for high school and college students. Students say the workshops provide tangible tools for greater confidence, clarity of mind and sense of belonging.

To sign up for a workshop, volunteer or learn more, visit:

www.artofliving.org   or   **us.yesplus.org**